NUFF SAID.

Chadd Wright

Photo credits: Chadd Wright

Cover Design by Chris Berge, Berge Design

ISBN: 9798874211110

*We have cashed in the instincts of our ancestors
to become excessively comfortable, overly anxious,
and mentally ill.*

*We have traded the ancient fear of cold and hunger
to become unwarranted cowards, afraid of our shadows.*

*We are raising a small army.
Those remaining who will change the tide and lead humanity
into a better future... please apply.*

NUFF SAID.

It is my endeavor when writing to squeeze the most meaning from the fewest words possible. It is a challenge, a sort of game I play. The title of this book and the words contained in it hopefully reflect that.

I also read a lot and cannot tolerate a writer who drones on about any given topic after the point has been articulated. That is another reason why I have written this way.

Each entry in this book is meant to be read individually and pondered by the reader. Each thought I have recorded contains a lesson or a point. Sometimes the lesson or point is very obvious, and sometimes it is more difficult to distinguish. Sometimes there will be more than one point. Sometimes, because your mind is not mine, you will see nothing of value.

The photographs contained in these pages will oftentimes correspond with the writing they are attached to. The image is meant to bring depth, context, and more meaning to the written words. Study it before you read each passage. Maybe you will see behind my eyes and deeper into the mind that penned the words.

Each of these chronological writings is a reflection of my mind during a certain time, in a specific place and circumstance. Volume I is obviously the beginning, and as you proceed to the end of this volume and on to the next, you will witness the time and circumstances of my life changing.

You will be joining me on my own personal journey of growth physically, mentally, and spiritually.

Enjoy the ride. Ask why. Learn from my failures and my success. Never quit. Always observe, think, and then act accordingly.

NUFF SAID.
Chadd Wright

Dangerous Achievements

Run. Run. Run.
The training is nearly finished.

The muscles feel like strands of sinew under the skin.
But most importantly, the mind has become calloused like the
hands of an old farmer, working day in and day out.

I have become obsessed.

This morning made 75 hard miles in 4.5 days.
I awoke to cold rain and a 35-degree temperature.
I donned my XOSKIN and went out to train anyways.
Is this normal?
It feels like nothing to me now.
My close friends, Discomfort and Pain, are ever present.

It is time to focus.
I spend time every day visualizing. This is so important,
equal to every hour spent physically preparing.

March 16, 2019

Victory is ours for the taking.
There are no problems, only situations that need solutions.

I do not say these things boastfully.
This is the essential mindset.
If you cannot view yourself as unbeatable, then you will
suffer defeat.

It is time to stay constantly aware of my self-talk, only
positive and on the verge of "cocky."
All negativity is shut out, whether in the form of music,
people, or situations.
There is validity in the concept of speaking things into
existence.

The training will continue, now only to get my daily dose of
discomfort.
There is danger in comfort when preparing for the task at
hand.
The only easy day was yesterday.
Does that make sense to you?

There is also danger in limiting myself by dwelling on past
achievements.
Yes, I have endured the hardest military training in the free
world.
I have run some hard races.
These things don't matter;
a ship does not sail on yesterday's wind.

I can only hope the challenge ahead will surpass all these
things.

NUFF SAID.

March 16, 2019

Get real.

There are days when I no longer know who I am.
So often I lose sight of where and what I came from.

How easy is it to forget the people and places who
shaped me,
loved me,
fed me,
believed in me.

I have a strange quality, I become completely consumed with
a task.
I suffer from total focus on a given challenge.
It often leads to victory, but at what cost?

A lonesome place, where you lose sight of your past and
future.
A false reality, unsustainable and ending in misery.

March 14, 2019

An inner weakness that from the outside is viewed as strength.
But there are people here who have known me from the beginning,
when I had nothing to show,
nothing to be proud of,
no great accomplishments or stories to tell.

I depend on these people to bring me back to level ground, to GET REAL with me when my views become abstract or go dark.

There are few remaining who know the real me.
Life has taken me many miles from them.

Today I am thankful for those few who have the knowledge and the courage to bring me back to base.

NUFF SAID.

What drives you forward once you reach the point in life that you have everything you could have ever dreamed of having?

It should be the same things that were driving you when you had nothing:

Purpose
Mission
Faith
Commitment
Dedication
Duty

Very few people will ever get the chance to realize this lesson.

NUFF SAID.

March 17, 2019

EXPLICIT

I don't talk much about my old job.

You won't find photographs of me wearing body armor,
carrying a weapon in some faraway place. They exist, but
only for me.

I have been around the world.
Shook hands with and protected the most powerful men on
earth.
All it did was confuse me.

So I ran back to my roots.
You might find it odd how I make my living these days.
Laugh if you will, but I have found happiness simply caring
for God's creation.

NUFF SAID.

BABYFACE

We thought these days were hard.
3rd phase, San Clemente Island.

Looking back, it was the most simplistic time of my adult
life.
I lived by one mantra, *Make it through the morning.*

Wake up. Get wet, sandy, and cold.
I could never find a reason to quit after the morning routine
was complete.
The hard part was done.

Now I just have to keep moving.

NUFF SAID.

May 29, 2019

SUFFER IN SILENCE

SEAL Qualification Training,
Close Quarters Combat, "Paying the man."
Look at that grimace.

Nowadays, I meet pain and discomfort with silence and a
straight face. They are respected but not feared.
A healthy dose of both is essential for our growth as humans.

Mind and muscle have become calloused after a decade of
accepting difficult tasks, a trait us country folks simply
describe as GRIT.

*Not only that, but we rejoice in our sufferings, knowing that
suffering produces endurance, and endurance produces
character, and character produces hope, and hope does not
put us to shame.**

NUFF SAID.

Romans 5:3-5 ESV

June 9, 2019

WARNING: LIFE AIN'T ALWAYS BEAUTIFUL.

Just think…
On the surface, this picture looks like another cool guy Navy
SEALs moment.
Let me tell you the real story, deeper than what your eyes can
see.

Standing beside me is my "sea daddy," my mentor when I
first arrived at the SEAL team.
He taught me the art of war, selflessly unwavering for
countless hours.

Daniel "Jake" Hubman was his name, and he took his own
life not long after this photo, broken inside from conflict and
duty.

You would have never known from this picture, huh?
So think before you compare your personal life to the false
reality portrayed on social media.

NUFF SAID.

June 12, 2019

BACK HOME

Yesterday I was on my hands and knees in the summer heat, pulling weeds from a flower bed for a stranger, drenched in dirt and sweat. It brought a smile to my face when I recalled standing by the bedside of the President of the United States while he slept soundly, knowing a sheepdog had the watch.

The sideways look of disgust from a pompous man with his false sense of superiority humors me.

Humble yourself daily. Choose a season to purposely accept the most minuscule tasks in view of others, because it is healthy for your soul.

It is good policy to treat everyone in our lives with respect. There might be more to the man who cuts your grass, fixes your plumbing, or collects your trash than meets the eye.

Why did Jesus get on His knees and wash the dirty feet of His disciples?

NUFF SAID.

MOTIVATION?

A "buzz" word in our society.
So many are searching for that something or someone to
motivate themselves.

Problem is, motivation is a fickle and fleeting thing driven by
daily emotion and external sources.

The more perfect question is, "How can I nourish the flame
that burns within my soul and spirit?"

When the body, soul (mind, will, emotions), and spirit are
healthy and in unison, we tap into a powerful and permanent
force, driving us forward in all aspects of life.

Practical, applicable skills delivered by the most complete
humans on earth, coming soon.

NUFF SAID.

June 25, 2019

IT DOESN'T MATTER.

It doesn't matter that we ran 50+ miles just for fun.

It doesn't matter that every joint in our bodies ached.

It doesn't matter that it was pouring rain all morning.

Nobody cares, nor should they.

A brotherhood forged by self-inflicted adversity,
realizing the power of positivity and the spoken word,
refusing to "Die in the chair,"
learning to "Suffer in silence."

THESE THINGS MATTER.

NUFF SAID.

June 29, 2019

WHAT MAKE US DIFFERENT?

How do we appreciate a sunrise, mesmerized by the sheer beauty and magnificence? How do we look up at the stars and begin to contemplate their vastness? How do we see the intricacy of nature?

Everything works in unison and complete harmony, designed by a master craftsman.

I have spent a LOT of time in nature, and I have never witnessed another animal stand mesmerized by the beauty surrounding them. So what makes us different?

For since the creation of the world God's invisible qualities— his eternal power and divine nature—have been clearly seen, being understood from what has been made, so that humans are without excuse. *

NUFF SAID.

Romans 1:20 NIV

August 1, 2019

ONE STEP AWAY

Every bone and muscle aches.
You haven't slept in over 96 hours.
You're freezing cold.
Sand and grit fill the bloody chafed areas between your legs
and under your arms.

There's the bell.

You think about the warm shower, hot meal, and restful sleep
that ringing the bell would usher in.

Lies.

There goes your friend.
Everyone around you is ringing the bell.
It mustn't be so bad.

There's the bell.

August 6, 2019

Ever present.
Mounted on the trailer hitch of a truck. Just one step away.

Screw that bell.
The temporary comfort it offers will destroy you and your dreams.
Refuse to even glance in its direction.

I will accept death before grasping its tassel and sending forth its sound.

This is life. Choose to hate the bell.

NUFF SAID.

SOMETIMES I make a mistake that humbles me.

SOMETIMES I need to be brought back to the present time and readjust my focus on the day God has given me.

SOMETIMES the people and things surrounding me suffer because of my selfishness.

SOMETIMES I forget that I am NOTHING without God's mercy, grace, forgiveness, and guidance.

ALWAYS He forgives me and shows me the most perfect way.

But you, O man of God, flee these things and pursue righteousness, godliness, faith, love, patience, gentleness. *

NUFF SAID.

1 Timothy 6:11 NKJV

August 12, 2019

A SHIP DOESN'T SAIL ON YESTERDAY'S WIND

Accomplish. Reflect.

Then shift, back to the drawing board.

Write your next chapter with boldness.

Steal your identity from the past and build upon it in the present and future.

Here lies life more abundantly:
*"I am come that they might have life, and that they might have it more abundantly."**

NUFF SAID.

John 10:10 KJV

A sound perspective is earned.

I know what I know, say the things I say,
because I chose not to surrender my helmet to this concrete
Grinder.

Although it is not enough for a man to accomplish only one
great task in life, I must continue to DO.

With every mission, knowledge and understanding of truth
grows. Perspective deepens.

I will only accept counsel from others in the arena, those
living, testing, proving, striving, doing.

"Counsel is mine, and sound wisdom;
I am understanding, I have strength." *

NUFF SAID.

Proverbs 8:14 NKJV

Myself...

I get tired.
I sometimes lose my path, winding through the forest of life.
I stumble and even fall.
I will never know it all.

I have an inexhaustible source of strength.
I have a compass and guiding light.
Angels bear me up on their wings.

I hold my truth and wisdom in the palm of my hands.
I answer my faults with these simple lines,
Not boastfully, but with Love,

Only to share what has worked for me during my journey.

NUFF SAID.

September 28, 2019

Life... Oh, Life.

What do you want from me?

I am but a simple man, simply blessed with the tools I need to find my way.
All I've ever needed are simple moments like this.

Yet there is quite obviously more. Keep the scales balanced until it's time to rest.

Honest scales and balances belong to the LORD; all the weights in the bag are of his making. *

NUFF SAID.

Proverbs 16:11 NIV

I was asked during a recent interview, "How do your spiritual beliefs help you when stuff gets hard?"

Easy answer.

I think about a man named Jesus, who walked thousands of miles to share love, then went willingly and was nailed to a wooden cross and hung until death.

He never uttered a single word of complaint.

Consider him who endured from sinners such hostility against himself, so that you may not grow weary or faint-hearted. In your struggle against sin you have not yet resisted to the point of shedding your blood.*

NUFF SAID.

*Hebrews 12:3-4 ESV

How many will never achieve their full potential…

It's a choice to take control of the incoming content that feeds my thoughts.

It's a choice to take control of the words that come out of my mouth.

I choose to Discipline myself, body, soul, and spirit.
Watch the right stuff,
listen to the right people,
learn from sound doctrine,
speak pure life and wisdom.

I will not utter excuses.
Own it, success and failure alike.

He who restrains his words has knowledge, And he who has a cool spirit is a man of understanding.*

NUFF SAID.

*Proverbs 17:27 NASB1995

December 1, 2019

I intentionally stay true to my roots, the foundation of hard manual labor and skills that shaped me as a young man.

My hands are better fitted to grip this heavy saw than to type these words.

Treat every good man with equal honor and respect.

Calloused hands and sun-burned skin might tell you more than an expensive suit and paperwork.

*As iron sharpens iron, So a man sharpens the countenance of his friend.**

NUFF SAID.

Proverbs 27:17 NKJV

I must remain constantly aware of complacency, especially on the downhill sections.

There are some things in life I cannot take back…
Bullets and Words are two.
I have learned both lessons the hard way.

I rarely slip and fall on an uphill trail.

Think.

NUFF SAID.

I will not rob myself of adventure by asking where the road leads.

Change the language from anxiety to excitement about the unknown.

Watch the path of your feet And all your ways will be established. *

NUFF SAID.

Proverbs 4:26 NASB1995

My roots are the anchor of all that I am today.

They run deep into the earth,
never changing,
awaiting my return.

Choose to never be ashamed.

*"He is like a tree planted by water,
that sends out its roots by the stream,
and does not fear when heat comes,
for its leaves remain green,
and is not anxious in the year of drought,
for it does not cease to bear fruit."*

NUFF SAID.

*Jeremiah 17:8 ESV

Opportunity must be followed by action.

Accept the risk.
Put in the work.
Embrace the unknown.

I choose to act upon opportunity presented to me, lest it slip
from my grasp.
This principle has led me to exotic lands, lifelong friendships,
and seemingly unattainable heights.

*"Behold, I stand at the door and knock. If anyone hears My
voice and opens the door, I will come in to him and dine with
him, and he with Me."**

NUFF SAID.

Revelation 3:20 NASB1995

My greatest moments are born,
my most valuable lessons are learned,
my strongest friendships are forged,
embarking on missions where "failure"
is the most likely outcome.

This is true adventure.

For I consider that the sufferings of this present time are not worthy to be compared with the glory which shall be revealed in us.

NUFF SAID.

Romans 8:18 NASB1995

Congenital pericardial cyst in a naval special warfare candidate; Clearance for diving after resection

BRENDAN T. BYRNE, M.D., LT MC (UMO/DMO) USN [1]; CHARLES C. FALZON, M.D., LT MC (UMO/DMO) USN[1]; PAUL D. JOHENK, D.O., LT MC (UMO/DMO) USN[1]; STEVEN C. ROMERO, M.D., LCDR MC (FS) USN[2]

[1] Naval Health Clinic Great Lakes, Division of Undersea Medicine;
[2] Naval Health Clinic Great Lakes, Division of Cardiology.

CORRESPONDING AUTHOR: Dr. Brendan Byrne – brendan.byrne@med.navy.mil

ABSTRACT

Introduction: We report the case of a 19-year-old male military recruit who presented for a screening physical for U.S. Naval Special Warfare and Diving Duty. During his screening physical examination, an exophytic pericardial cyst was discovered. Subsequent work-up revealed normal cardiopulmonary function despite this large 7-cm mass, but the candidate was disqualified due to concerns regarding the risk of complications. He underwent successful elective surgical resection without post-operative complications. One year post-operatively, he repeated his cardiopulmonary work-up with normal results and successfully completed training.

Methods: Literature search was conducted using PubMed/Medline. Keywords included pericardial/um, cyst, mediastinum, special operations, military, diving, thoracoscopy/ic resection. Results that included cases of pericardial cysts or other mediastinal tumors were included.

Results: Review of the literature reveals that complications are rare and range widely in severity. Analysis of the physiology of diving, together with absence of reported cases, suggest that there is little to no increased risk in recreational scuba diving for subjects with asymptomatic lesions. While no cases of morbidity or mortality have been reported in elite athletes, the severe and repetitive trauma experienced by Special Operators raises clinical concern for these lesions.

Conclusion: Because of the increased risk of morbidity and mortality in the Special Operations environment, clearance for duty should not be granted those individuals. However, in the general population, as well as with low-impact activities such as recreational scuba diving, periodic observation without resection seems reasonable.

INTRODUCTION

Congenital pericardial cysts are benign mesothelial-cell-lined neoplasms arising from the pericardium itself. Non-congenital etiologies include infectious (*e.g.*, echinococcal cysts) and inflammatory cysts (secondary to trauma or surgical intervention, pericarditis, effusions that become loculated, as well as pseudocysts). They are generally benign structures that measure from 1 to 28 centimeters (cm) in diameter and are filled with clear transudative fluid (hence the earlier eponym, spring water cysts) [1,2,6].

In the general population, the commonly accepted therapeutic approach is observation in the case of asymptomatic cysts, and thorascopic resection for symptomatic lesions only [1,2,3,4,6].

Infectious, traumatic or inflammatory cysts can present significant morbidity, usually related to their etiology. In contrast, congenital pericardial cysts rarely cause clinically significant symptoms unless they grow to such a size as to cause involvement with surrounding structures, or pose increased risk of rupture. This is more common in the setting of an endophytic pericardial cyst, as opposed to the more common exophytic form, that by definition grows outside the pericardial sac [1,2,6].

Symptoms from larger cysts are generally mild, such as a persistent cough, but complications have been described that include death, cardiac tamponade, erosion of the myocardium, shock, life-threatening hemorrhage and tracheobronchial obstruction [12-23].

So many people have asked me about this. So here it is, straight from the medical journal, sent to me this day by a US Navy Dive Medical Officer. The story of a young Navy SEAL candidate undergoing elective heart surgery to accomplish his dream.

Never let the opinions of others dictate your time, speed, and direction.
NUFF SAID.

January 27, 2020

I still remember my last day of high school, begging my teachers to change my grades so I could graduate. For some reason, they did. Maybe they saw something in me that I did not know existed.

It was a long journey, getting from there to the moment this picture was taken.

I learned to embrace every second. I own the mistakes and successes alike. I can now see clearly, every decision was leading me to this specific moment.

Until the end comes, I trust the design.

"Before I formed you in the womb I knew you; Before you were born I sanctified you; I ordained you a prophet to the nations."*

NUFF SAID.

*Jeremiah 1:5 NKJV

February 4, 2020

In my days I have witnessed the lives of strong men
shatter in an instant.
I sit sleepless tonight, asking my God,
Why have you preserved me?

I am encouraged to remain steadfast along my path.

There are questions with answers I could never comprehend.

Front sight focused.

*For the vision is yet for an appointed time, but at the end it
shall speak, and not lie: though it tarry, wait for it; because it
will surely come. **

NUFF SAID.

*Habakkuk 2:3 KJV

February 6, 2020

What is this flesh that screams
what I should or should not do?
It consistently begs for pleasure.
It is only self-seeking.
Perpetual comfort is its request.
In the morning it whispers for more sleep.
In the cold it complains for warmth.
In the wet its only thought is to get dry.
At mealtime it craves more food than necessary.
On the run it asks me to stop short of my goal.
In life it yearns after lustful thoughts.

Heed the flesh and destruction will swiftly follow.
Deny yourself, that the flesh might realize it is but a vessel.

For if you live according to the flesh you will die; but if by the Spirit you put to death the deeds of the body, you will live. *

NUFF SAID.

Romans 8:13 NKJV

February 11, 2020

Your direction is not always clear.

Take up your tools,
study the available routes,
calculate your bearings and Continue Mission.

The decision to act will always lead you closer to the
objective than the alternative.

The principle implies initiative.
Refuse to crouch in stagnant fear awaiting instructions that
might never come.

*And I say unto you, Ask, and it shall be given you; seek, and
ye shall find; knock, and it shall be opened unto you.* *

NUFF SAID.

Luke 11:9 KJV

February 16, 2020

Control thyself.

There are only so many excuses I can give and only so many excuses you can take.
The day has not yet dawned when I couldn't muster enough strength to rise up off my couch.

I'm talking reality, not some self-imagined view.

I arrive to the arena, never the strongest, rarely the fastest, seldom the smartest.
But I ARRIVE.

Don't drag me to the starting line.
Use your valuable time on those who got there themselves.

Some will understand this, some will not.
Soft delivery of a hard message.

NUFF SAID.

February 19, 2020

Take quitting off the table.

Take fear out of the equation.

Take the power away from anxiety.

I will Charlie Mike (Continue Mission) until I achieve victory or something outside of my control changes my direction.

With this tool I simplify the potential outcome of every situation.

For we wrestle not against flesh and blood. *

NUFF SAID.

Ephesians 6:12 KJV

March 6, 2020

He shall continuously renew my strength.
I shall mount up with wings like eagles.

I shall run and not be weary.
I shall walk and not faint.

I shall not fear.
I shall not be dismayed.

I shall prosper and have peace.

I shall make these affirmations with boldness. Standing upon these promises.

He who dwells in the shelter of the Most High will abide in the shadow of the Almighty.

NUFF SAID.

Psalm 91:1 ESV

March 8, 2020

She doesn't need to look at a cell phone.
She doesn't have to check her Inbox.

She is not concerned with timelines.
She is not impressed by material things.

She melts my heart like nothing else on this earth.
She is more pure and beautiful than any sunrise or
mountaintop.

She reminds me of the order of life.
She restores my soul.

*"Let the little children come to me, and do not hinder them,
for the kingdom of heaven belongs to such as these."* *

NUFF SAID.

*Matthew 19:14 NIV

We control the fear.
The fear does not control us.

Lift up your head.
Care for your fellow man.

The sun will rise and set. Provision resides in nature.
Take only what you need for today;
selfish hoarding cannot weather the storm.

Distance only feeds discontent.

There are two possible outcomes for every new day.

For God hath not given us the spirit of fear, but of power, and of love, and of a sound mind.*

NUFF SAID.

*2 Timothy 1:7 NKJV

A Slower Pace

I have been taking the opportunity to reconnect with passions from my childhood, things like fly fishing, riding a bicycle, getting my hands in the dirt—

simple yet grounded forms of activity that have been lost in the shuffle of adult life for over two decades.

It's so rewarding to feel the old channels of my soul reawaken.

Rejoice, O young man, in your youth, And let your heart cheer you in the days of your youth. *

NUFF SAID.

Ecclesiastes 11:9 NKJV

Take quitting off the table.

It's so simple.
Continue to push forward, relentlessly, in the direction of your goal until something outside of your control either stops you or changes your direction.

Why fear tomorrow if you've decided not to quit?

Why have anxiety about the outcome if you know you're pushing to your limit?

I witnessed many men choose to complicate a simple evolution called Navy SEAL Training by leaving quitting as an option.

For temporary comfort they ran to the bell and gave up their dreams.

Don't be that guy.

And let us not grow weary of doing good, for in due season we will reap, if we do not give up. *

NUFF SAID.

*Galatians 6:9 ESV

I am humbly your servant.
I will gladly become less, that you may become more.

I pour myself out daily,
Sustained by rivers of living water.

For though I preach the gospel, I have nothing to glory of:
for necessity is laid upon me; yea, woe is unto me, if I preach
not the gospel!*

NUFF SAID.

*1 Corinthians 9:16 KJV

April 3, 2020

Can you handle it?
If the world was your footstool, could you remain
true to yourself?

Here lies the struggle for most.

The desire to "prove" myself to others will only ever
limit my potential.

I have no great desire for influence, yet opportunity is set in
my path.
I have no longing for possessions, yet all my needs are met.
I have nothing to prove, yet I continue to accomplish.

Completeness was born out of submission and humility.
A true sense of freedom was achieved in acceptance.
Riches were found in a place of release.

*Do nothing from rivalry or conceit, but in humility count
others more significant than yourselves.* *

NUFF SAID.

Philippians 2:3 ESV

April 10, 2020

How can I actually believe…
that two thousand years ago my Creator sent His "Son" to
earth to reconcile me unto Him?

How can I actually believe…
that this "Son" of God lived an absolutely perfect and pure
life, bringing His flesh into total subjection, overcoming all
sin and temptation?

How can I actually believe…
that this "Son" of God was named Jesus, and that He so
desired to redeem me from my inherent lack of righteousness
that He went willingly to a cross in order to cover my iniquity
and perpetual sin?

How can I actually believe…
that this Jesus rose from the dead on the third day after His
crucifixion, giving *me* eternal victory over death, hell,
and the grave?

April 12, 2020

How can I actually believe…
that this Jesus is seated at the right hand of God the Father
today, making intercession for me?

I believe… only by the grace of God. My "measure" of faith
is my most precious possession and valuable gift.

I believe… because I was literally transformed overnight.
I believe… because He opened my eyes to the unerring truth
of His Word.
I believe… because I have experienced His forgiveness
and guidance.

I believe… because He chose to reveal Himself to me and I
chose to submit to His kingship.
I believe… because I don't have to look far to be reminded of
His magnificence.

I'm not asking you to believe.
That's impossible, in my opinion.

All I can say is,
*"Ask and it will be given to you; seek and you will find; knock
and the door will be opened to you."**

NUFF SAID.

Matthew 7:7 NIV

April 12, 2020

I could never forget the horrific stench of this place, searing my nostrils and lungs with every breath.

Children, scooting across broken pavement, crippled with poliovirus and other debilitating illnesses forgotten by the first world.

After dark it was a guaranteed case of malaria, dengue, or yellow fever.

Sanitation was nonexistent.
Law and order were not even a thought.

These people still managed to live their lives in relative happiness and contentment.
Most had a beautiful faith and kind smile in the midst of death and destruction.

April 15, 2020

Who am I to ever be ungrateful in a place where we get to choose between good and better?

Thank God for these memories that keep me conscious of what "could" be.

NUFF SAID.

Green helmets lined the Grinder.
This was a shrine left by all the men who chose to quit.

The line grew longer every day.

They say there are two possible human reactions in the
furnace of adversity—
fight or flight.

God didn't give me wings.

NUFF SAID.

The true depth of darkness is known only by those who endure long enough to see the dawn break.

The piercing cold reaches its pinnacle just before the sun takes its sharpness away.

Don't cheat yourself. Light is about to break the horizon.

Principles of nature

*Weeping may endure for a night, But joy comes in the morning.**

NUFF SAID.

Psalm 30:5 NKJV

Now prepare yourself like a man;
I will question you, and you shall answer me.

Have you an arm like God?
Or can you thunder with a voice like His?

Why do you not accept your burden and carry its weight with
contentment and courage until the night is finished?

Were you there when God laid the foundations of the Earth?

Why do you flee from the path that has been chosen for you
when the ground becomes unleveled?

Tell me, if you have understanding.

Will growth exist if you never allow adversity to run its
course?

NUFF SAID.

April 24, 2020

Something is stirring deep within.
I will continue to create, to build, to strive, to thrive
in the face of all odds.

I have a vision:

The arena will be filled
under the banner of
Hope
Courage
Love
Joy
Freedom
Christ.

NUFF SAID.

April 30, 2020

Never allow the fear to creep in.

Like many of you guys, we have taken a big financial hit over the last two months.
The fear tries to creep in.

I recall the evening this photo was taken. We were getting ready to launch off this pier into the murky water for a combat diving mission, one of the most dangerous and complex skills we practiced as Navy SEALs.

The fear tried to creep in.

I later found myself 20 feet deep, underneath a massive vessel, trying to navigate through complete darkness with no way to reach the surface if an emergency occurred.

The fear tried to creep in.

May 16, 2020

I remember hearing a gargling sound in my Drager LAR V, signaling there was water leaking into my breathing loop, creating a caustic cocktail of chemicals that could potentially be sucked down my throat with the next breath.

The fear tried to creep in.

I remember checking my depth gauge, wondering if I had taken too many excursions to depths where the oxygen I was breathing becomes toxic.

The fear tried to creep in.

I remember thinking, *If I panic right now, I will likely die or get severely injured.*

The consequences are catastrophic if we allow the fear to creep in.

NUFF SAID.

I am vexed.
Complexities abound, unsearchable by the shallow depth of
the human mind.

There is One within me who has conquered the world, death,
hell, and the grave.
To Him I will run. I will be His standard bearer.
He shall preserve the love within my heart and build a hedge
around my soul.

Come what may, I will remain standing,
propped up by grace, mercy, forgiveness, love,
and a strength that is not my own.

My King is totally righteous and never changing.

Pierce the darkness with pure unfailing light,

*For dust thou art, and unto dust shalt thou
return.* *

May 31, 2020

Spare me from your opinions.
Keep your offering.
Look up. The King is coming.

*"And because lawlessness will abound, the love of many will grow cold. But he who endures to the end shall be saved."**

NUFF SAID.

Genesis 3:19 KJV, Matthew 24:12-13 NKJV

Nothing Left

A friend of mine sent me this picture today.

This is the result of 116.5 miles of continuous running
through every element nature could muster against me.

A hollow shell, stripped down to only the most primal
instincts. Sleep and breathe.

From this hollow shell, I rebuild.
Every time I have rebuilt, the shell has become stronger
inside and out.

I empty my vessel through tribulation willingly,
leaving everything on the battlefield of life,
for I have discovered the glorious result.

NUFF SAID.

June 5, 2020

A message to my enemy—

You cannot rattle me.

You are the creator of confusion.
You are the source of strife.
You are the author of lies.
You sustain the spirit of fear.

You cannot rattle me.

I have trodden upon foreign lands
where all things have been shaken,
yet I remain steady,
poised,
at peace,
unwavering.

June 8, 2020

Waste your precious enticement elsewhere.

You cannot rattle me.

"And the rain fell, and the floods came, and the winds blew and beat on that house, but it did not fall, because it had been founded on the rock."*

NUFF SAID.

*Matthew 7:25 ESV

I am a warrior by trade.

It is a rare opportunity in this life to battle against a truly worthy opponent.

Greg Armstrong IS that man. He forced me to grow. He prayed over me. He gave me strength. He demonstrated the finest example of human will and never-quit mentality.

Today I am thankful for the brothers and sisters that I get to share this life with.

Today I am thankful for the support and encouragement that each and every one of you guys gave me during this mission.

Today I am thankful that Marq Brown and Jesse Itzler stood by my side, every step, caring for me and capturing the essence of the battle perfectly.

June 22, 2020

Today I am thankful for my faith in Jesus Christ, who sustains me daily through His presence and principles.

Today I am thankful to Becca Jones and Jon Cox for intentionally prepping the battlefield and providing a place for us humans to sharpen one another.

Today I take a moment to reflect.

Tomorrow, I focus my attention on the next summit that awaits.

NUFF SAID.

Be patient.
There is a process we all must endure.

This weekend at Mid-State Mile there were 26 hours of patience preceding 4 hours of growth.

You can't cheat it.
You can't go around it.
There is no other way.

Without patience victory cannot be achieved.

*Rejoice in hope, be patient in tribulation, be constant in prayer.**

NUFF SAID.

Romans 12:12 ESV

Inexhaustible strength.

It started and ended in prayer,
warriors making intercession for one another.

Take heed to men knit together with heavenly bonds!

Never confuse meekness for weakness.

Likewise the Spirit helps us in our weakness. For we do not know what to pray for as we ought, but the Spirit himself intercedes for us with groanings too deep for words.*

NUFF SAID.

*Romans 8:26 ESV

The Process of Recovery

I pour out my heart and soul,
sacrificing my very flesh for the greater good,
that one day my life may be looked upon
as a worthy example.

"Normal" life is in danger of losing its color.

I climb this mountain to intentionally watch the magnificence
of a sunset.

The vividness of creation tells me there is no such thing as
"normal" life—
I am surrounded by a miracle.

My lens becomes crystal clear.

NUFF SAID.

June 26, 2020

The standard of excellence:

I will crank these pedals just a little faster,
I will move my feet just a little quicker,
I will be just a little more patient,
I will be just a little mentally stronger,
I will be just a little physically harder,
I will be just a little more deliberate.

The difference between mediocrity and excellence
is "just a little."

NUFF SAID.

June 28, 2020

I will be hungry for excellence in victory and defeat.

I will be willing to walk through the furnace of adversity to earn my growth and perspective.

I will remain humble, serving those around me with a pure heart, expecting nothing in return.

I will conduct myself with honor on and off the battlefield of life.

I will practice self-control regardless of circumstance.

My integrity will remain steadfast and unwavering.

I will stand ready to lead myself, my team, and my family, always by example.

June 30, 2020

I will demand discipline, bringing all aspects of my body, soul, and spirit into subjection.

I will be innovative, adjusting my thoughts, actions, and words to accomplish my current mission.

I am never out of the fight.

NUFF SAID.

Blurry

I spit a stream of tobacco juice on the freshly polished boot of my teammate.
Strife had been brewing between him and me for months.

The next morning, I awake to find my only pair of boots
filled to the brim with fine sand from the pristine beaches of
San Clemente Island.

I need not ask who the culprit was.

He challenges me in full view of the whole class, a footrace
up Al Huey (a brutal .5-mile-long hill leading out the back of
our barracks).

We settle our differences as men in BUD/S.

Everyone knew he was fast, coming in first place nearly
every evolution throughout SEAL Training.

July 3, 2020

In contrast, I had purposely never been first.
Never.

The deal was sealed in everyone's eyes;
I was about to be crushed and humiliated.

But... the Gray Man was about to show his cards.

We shot off the line, young muscle striving in the heat of
extracurricular competition.

He cannot win against me.
I knew the whole time that he could not win, but why spoil a
good show?

Feint weakness in the eyes of your competition, and deliver
the crushing blow once the stage is set.

NUFF SAID.

July 3, 2020

There are two sides.

They exist in harmony; both are necessary.

One side exists in order to keep the other alive.
One side must be fed, the other kept hungry.
One side is understood, the other taboo.

A shadow is cast in the presence of light.
Complexity not easily understood.
The burden is mine.

Warrior by trade.

He has inscribed a circle on the face of the waters at the boundary between light and darkness. *

NUFF SAID.

Job 26:10 ESV

July 16, 2020

Continued Assessment

You have a choice to make:
Will you become an asset or a liability?

There is no in-between.

The team can only carry a liability so far until it collapses internally.

Don't be ashamed to trim the fat within your circle.

Carry your weight.

NUFF SAID.

My biggest smiles are usually inspired by God's creatures.

Peace, love, calmness, and trust are contagious,
on display in their purest form in nature.

The horse doesn't care how many followers I have.
She respects me because of her keen sense of who I am.

NUFF SAID.

"All we've got to do is execute the plan."

What if I told you I was at a very low point when this clip was captured?
Understand one thing: It's easy to throw your plan out the window when life gets hard.

Winners execute the plan.
Period.
The level of difficulty and discomfort is irrelevant.

There was a plan when I started this race.
There was a plan when I married my wife.
There was a plan when I started SEAL Training.
There was a plan when I started my business.

I execute the plan. Hour after hour. Day after day.

NUFF SAID.

July 25, 2020

IT PAYS TO BE A WINNER

A principle engrained so deeply into everything I put my hands to;
a principle foreign in the haze of modern society;
a principle that has applied since the dawn of mankind;
a principle that will make you push harder, faster, farther;
a principle that reaps reward.

Never settle.

IT PAYS TO BE A WINNER

Do you not know that in a race all the runners run, but only one receives the prize? So run that you may obtain it. *

NUFF SAID.

1 Corinthians 9:24 ESV

I will never be bound up by my possessions.

Material wealth can lead to a life of passive slavery.

The old ways are not lost to me.

*"No one can serve two masters."**

NUFF SAID.

Matthew 6:24 NKJV

Work every angle.
Strike from cover.
Minimize the effectiveness of your opponent's weapons.
Take every advantage away from your enemies.

My goal is not simply victory.
I will win smartly,
rising above my competition unscathed.

Warrior by trade.

NUFF SAID.

August 9, 2020

The concept of individual liberty is founded upon a single principle,

Love your neighbor as you love yourself.

98% of the "hot topic" debates we're having as a society seem ridiculous in light of this principle.

Strive to achieve a REALITY wherein you TRULY love yourself.

Strife, temptation, and hate fade away.

And the second is like unto it, Thou shalt love thy neighbour as thyself.*

NUFF SAID.

*Matthew 22:39 KJV

How long will you cheat?
Until you become enslaved by your quick fix?

You don't like your reality?
Put in the hard yards and create one you love.

You don't like your body?
Get in trenches and build the one you're proud of.

You don't like your job?
Burn the midnight oil and emerge victorious.

There is no sustainable handout.

You can keep the snake oil, drugs, and sympathy.
I'll take the hard road. Every time.

NUFF SAID.

August 26, 2020

The tides are about to change.

I shy away from predictions;
I release any expectations.

I trust the Intuition provided by the sovereign God
I seek and serve.
There is no possibility of failure.

I am upheld by the Creator,
the Author and Finisher,
the Alpha and Omega,
the First and the Last.

I'm not interested in second place.

You want to run your race with intensity and confidence
humanly impossible?
*"Seek first the kingdom of God and His righteousness, and all
these things shall be added to you."* *

September 8, 2020

I didn't say attend church every Sunday.
I didn't say place your hope in human teachers.
I didn't say seek some super-spiritual experience.
I didn't say judge the hypocrisy within the body of Christ.
I didn't say the path was going to be easy.

I said,
*"Seek first the kingdom of God and His righteousness, and all these things shall be added to you."**

Can you read? Pick up the Book.
Can you breathe? Lift up praise unto Him.
Can you see? Follow the example of Jesus.
Can you hear? Set aside your pride and open your ears to the voice of freedom, truth, and understanding.

NUFF SAID.

Matthew 6:33 NKJV

I was asked, "How do you stay so motivated?"
Such a simple question to answer.

Realization of my true capability created an unquenchable
thirst to achieve.
A human who finally grasps the depths of their potential
is unstoppable.

What if I told you that this realization is the only difference
between you and I?

What if I told you this simple concept is the key
to limitless heights?

What if I told you it's impossible for me to fail because
God's Word has revealed this truth to me?

Would you believe me?

NUFF SAID.

September 14, 2020

Satisfaction is not hinged upon a desired result.

True fulfillment is achieved by adherence to the principles
I have sworn to uphold.

Remember this in the furnace of adversity,
when the result is uncertain,
when the finish line is nowhere to be seen.

Sleep soundly, knowing you didn't compromise your
integrity for the sake of temporary comfort.

NUFF SAID.

September 20, 2020

I don't teach from theory.

Sift me like sand,
you will find struggle, failure, success, victory, and loss.

Never be so foolish as to accept a title "The Toughest Man Alive."

To stay on the ground level means victory and defeat
are ever present.

On the ground level, our currency is mud, sweat, blood,
and tears of joy and sadness.

NUFF SAID.

HONOR
(The adherence to what is right)

How do we conduct ourselves with HONOR in an
environment where the lines between right and wrong are
blurred, nearly unrecognizable?

I have found it hard at times to stand upon what I know is
right, almost guilted into a place of submission and
acceptance of lawlessness.

Know that YOU HAVE BEEN SET APART.

The fact that your conscience still reins you back to truth and
light indicates the battle is not lost.

Finding a foundation of uncompromising moral truth is the
first step of establishing HONOR in life.

September 27, 2020

Agendas change, times change, people change. Right and wrong never change.

"And pay your vows to the Most High;
Call upon Me in the day of trouble;
*I will rescue you, and you will honor Me."**

NUFF SAID.

Psalm 50:14-15 NASB

The presence of struggle is indicative of hope.

Are you not satisfied with your current self?
There is hope.

Do you dislike your habits?
There is hope.

Are you striving to break the bonds of some hidden sin?
There is hope.

Are you searching for positive change and growth?
There is hope.

Hope dies with the acceptance of our imperfections.
*And even as they did not like to retain God in their
knowledge, God gave them over to a debased mind, to do
those things which are not fitting.* *

NUFF SAID.

Romans 1:28 NKJV

September 28, 2020

Warning: Emotions are poor leaders.

Let me introduce you to a fundamental problem of society.
Feast your eyes on an entire population being led astray by
"leaders" who follow their emotions.
Take a look at a majority of citizenship who follow their
emotions.

Following your emotions will lead you to:
1. Inconsistency
2. Irrational behavior
3. Moral decay
4. Confusion
5. Ultimately, a life without vision paired with imperceptible
lines between right and wrong.

How about following sound principles that are proven on the
battlefield of life?

How about following logic?

October 1, 2020

How about making your emotions serve you instead of becoming servants to them?

Give it a try. I guarantee you, it will work.

Where there is no vision, the people perish: but he that keepeth the law, happy is he.*

NUFF SAID.

*Proverbs 29:18 KJV

What would you have done differently today if you knew failure was impossible?

Abundant life awaits all those who crush the fear of failure.

For the righteous falls seven times and rises again, but the wicked stumble in times of calamity. *

I CANNOT FAIL.

"For I know the plans I have for you, declares the LORD, plans for welfare and not for evil, to give you a future and a hope." *

I CANNOT FAIL.

Trust in the LORD with all your heart, and do not lean on your own understanding. In all your ways acknowledge him, and he will make straight your paths. *

October 6, 2020

I CANNOT FAIL.

Cast your burden on the LORD, and he will sustain you; he will never permit the righteous to be moved.*

I CANNOT FAIL.

The steps of a man are established by the LORD, when he delights in his way; though he fall, he shall not be cast headlong, for the LORD upholds his hand.*

I CANNOT FAIL

"Have I not commanded you? Be strong and courageous. Do not be frightened, and do not be dismayed, for the LORD your God is with you wherever you go."*

I CANNOT FAIL

And I am sure of this, that he who began a good work in you will bring it to completion at the day of Jesus Christ.*

I CANNOT FAIL

NUFF SAID.

*Proverbs 24:16, Jeremiah 29:11, Proverbs 3:5-6, Psalm 55:22, Psalm 37:23-24, Joshua 1:9, Philippians 1:6, all ESV

I don't care who's watching.

External recognition will never dictate the intensity of my effort.

You don't need to see the thousands of hours of work it took.

You don't need to see the never-ending flights, sleeping on a cold steel aircraft floor coming home from some third-world country.

You don't need to see the millions of repetitions.

You don't need to see the thousands of lonesome miles.

You don't need to see months away from home while my loved ones suffered, not knowing if I would return.

October 13, 2020

You don't need to see the sadness. The suffering. The pure grit. The failures. The tenacity. The hate. The uncertainty.

Or maybe you do… just to make you realize this journey is no joke and nothing is free.

So pick up your strength and understand why I am who I am.

Adjust your expectations or put in the work. No matter who's watching.

It is the ONLY way.

NUFF SAID.

P.S. Don't just be a consumer. Pass the freakin' word!

October 13, 2020

YOU have the answers to 98% of the problems you will encounter in life

YOU have been equipped with the most powerful mind on Planet Earth.

YOU have been empowered to take dominion over your surroundings.

YOU have two options. Stay crouched in stagnant fear, or make a decision and hopefully win the fight.

Victory requires action.
Action creates momentum.
Momentum gives birth to liberty.

"Give me liberty or give me death."

NUFF SAID.

October 21, 2020

If you continue to think like an individual, you will continue to fail.
Guaranteed.

Life will keep dragging your butt through the mud until you make the mental shift from "me-me-me" to "team-team-team."

The quickest way to be labeled a turd in the SEAL teams was to think like an individual.

Get out of your own little head and realize your failure is likely rooted in a choice you've made to be a selfish consumer instead of a powerful contributor.

NUFF SAID.

P.S. Never ring the bell.

October 27, 2020

Plan your dive, dive your plan.

Calculate the time, speed, and distance to your objective.

Map the most efficient route from point A to B.

Identify the obstacles in between.

When it gets dark, cold, and nasty, stay the course.

When the unexpected happens, adapt, overcome, and return to your intended track.

Never allow fleeting emotions to override a scheme based on sound principles and intelligence.

NUFF SAID.

October 28, 2020

Commence Assault

We are standing in the threshold.
Go into the world and commence a full-frontal assault on the
gates of hell.

Call the hidden things into the light. Expose the darkness with
boldness.

You will know a tree by its fruit.
Ask yourself, "What are the fruits of the moral and ethical
decisions we're making as a society?"
What are the fruits of the individuals from whom you're
seeking counsel?

I'll take 20,000 committed warriors over 2 million lukewarm
followers.

October 29, 2020

There is but one way to experience permanent change and freedom. All other paths are ancillary.

*"So if the Son sets you free, you will be free indeed."**

NUFF SAID.

P.S. PASS THE WORD!

John 8:26 NIV

Divide and conquer,
an effective tactic older than history itself.

I am a tactician by trade.
My younger years were spent studying strategies used to take
control of a battlefield and dominate an enemy: Let's take the
high ground. Identify your target. Move and communicate
with each other.

Where do you stand? Make a choice today.

Become an asset to your nation, your family, your team.
Stifle your complaints. Take ownership. Shift fire. Win the
fight.

Tune out the rhetoric of cowards, lest you be drawn down
into their valley of despair.

DIVIDE AND CONQUER... just chew on that for a minute.

NUFF SAID.

November 8, 2020

Locate your exact position on the map.
Take a bearing to your destination.
Study the obstacles in-between.
Trust your compass.

I still get off course some days.
The micro terrain isn't illustrated by the contour lines of life.

Beware, lest the seemingly small things subconsciously
funnel you into a dark valley, choked with brush.

NUFF SAID.

November 14, 2020

You can't cash my checks.

I have signed a check payable for an amount up to and including my life.

I'll never forget the feeling. So few know the level of commitment involved.

There has never been a plan B.

Maybe that's why I'm so ardently opposed to the pandering of fools lacking allegiance, loyalty, direction, and devotion.

Is your flag firmly planted on the rock of truth?
Have the lines been drawn between right and wrong?

November 25, 2020

Choosing to neglect these essential decisions leads to a life absent of honor.

I would still sacrifice everything for the adherence to what is right.

And for this cause God shall send them strong delusion, that they should believe a lie.*

NUFF SAID.

*2 Thessalonians 2:11 KJV

PEACE AND SAFETY,
the new battle cry of humanity.

The deep lines on my face, the scars on my body,
the muscles forged stronger than sinew,
were not developed seeking peace and safety.

I don't have a single story or piece of wisdom attributed to
the quest for peace and safety.

Free nations were not established by men and women living
in peace and safety.

Life itself and all great achievement demands risk and
turbulence.

November 27, 2020

What will we sacrifice in order to achieve the ruse of peace and safety?

*For when they shall say, Peace and safety; then sudden destruction cometh upon them, as travail upon a woman with child; and they shall not escape.**

NUFF SAID.

*1 Thessalonians 5:3 KJV

The things that I do might look hard to you.
These things that you see are the ones that come easy to me.

My struggle is much different—
a video call in a cold, empty room,
my weapons moved or unorganized,
lack of a designated safe space,
the feeling of being uprooted.

I checked out of that life nearly two years ago.
That life didn't check out of me.

Circumstance sometimes brings old memories to bear.

NUFF SAID.

December 15, 2020

The words Motivation and Discipline no longer resonate with me.

Mission success must become integrated with your lifestyle and purpose.
The terms of your existence and momentum should never be dictated by fickle rules and emotions.

Honor, commitment, tenacity, courage, wisdom, confidence, and humility will produce success ONLY when paired with decades of relentless forward motion.

Just keep showing up.
Do the best you can.
One day, after everyone searching for the shortcut quits,
you'll be the only one left
and to the victor goes the spoils.

There… now you have the "secret to success."

NUFF SAID.

December 17, 2020

Hard times create strong men.
Strong men create good times.
Good times create weak men.
Weak men create hard times.

Sleep soundly, my friends.
We have the watch.

There are thousands like me,
created for those fleeing moments when light and darkness
intermingle, that golden hour when our enemy's movement
can only be seen through peripheral vision.

While the untrained person's gaze is fixed upon the obvious
distraction,
a warrior never stares directly at his prey.

NUFF SAID.

December 18, 2020

Leadership: A ridiculously over-complicated topic that sells books and gets speaking engagements.

Hold the phone. Let me give you the essence of leadership: "The courage and ability to make decisions."

So why are leaders so rare?
Because the simple task of making decisions carries the weight of accountability… and weak humans shirk that weight.

NUFF SAID.

Wealth equals security… in a world of illusion.

So we're taught to spend a lifetime acquiring material things alone. They serve as a facade to a shallow existence.

The small portion of security found in humanity is only achieved by building a net worth of life experience.

I have spent my days amassing a fortune of stories, places, memories, knowledge, friendships, faith, and truth.
Willingly enduring hardship, my deposits have been made in possessions of true value.
You can't cash my checks.
I lack nothing.

Do not set your mind on high things, but associate with the humble. *

NUFF SAID.

*Romans 12:16 NKJV

December 28, 2020

I am not a product of random circumstance.

Nothing irks me more than a defeatist mindset,
"Woe is me,"
"This is the hand I was dealt,"
"I'll never have the life I want because of my misfortune."

I do what Chadd wants to do.
Every day.
Because I did the hard yards that no one else wants to do.
Every day. For over a decade.

Life is unfair to the timid;
Fortune favors the bold.

You are a product of the circumstance you created.

NUFF SAID.

December 31, 2020

Anything less than this moment is a foolish desire.

My righteousness is as filthy rags in light of this child.

I'll never tell you what I think you want to hear.
I'll always tell you what I think you need to hear.
A poor salesman I am.

And he said: "Truly I tell you, unless you change and become like little children, you will never enter the kingdom of heaven." *

NUFF SAID.

Matthew 18:3 NIV

I view the action of fools with contempt, not concern.
The folly and ignorance of unorganized and reprobate
humans doesn't captivate my interest.

My gaze is fixed on the remaining few who are hungry for
improvement, truth, understanding, wisdom, and strength—
things eternal.

I spend my precious time forging warriors,
individuals who still have the courage to show up.
On time. On target. Ready to train.

These are the ones who matter to me.

Graduates of The Proving Ground-1 Troop, I salute you.

NUFF SAID.

January 11, 2021

How selfish to think your faith in Christ is given solely for your benefit.

Are you scared to be considered a fool?
*For the message of the cross is foolishness to those who are perishing.**

Do you think you're not qualified?
*God chose what is low and despised in the world, even things that are not, to bring to nothing things that are.**

No one stuck in an individualistic mindset will partake of the fruits of the Kingdom during this life.
Some things are bigger than YOU.

Be ready. Preach the word. Convince. Rebuke. Exhort.
Endure. Fulfill your Ministry.

NUFF SAID.

1 Corinthians 1:18 NIV, 1 Corinthians 1:28 ESV

January 18, 2021

There is no substitute for putting boots on the ground.

There is no replacement for cold air burning the lungs.

There is no exchange for the primal emotions felt when the tracks of a mountain lion are spotted crossing your trail.

There is no surrogate for the true sense of aloneness.

This ain't no Zoom call.

NUFF SAID.

Your pain is not unique to you.

This is me… yes me, after my very first ultra marathon.

Yes, I suffer.
Your suffering does not make you special.

Yes, I feel pain.
Your pain does not make you unique.

Yes, I have days when I'm depressed.
Your depression does not make you distinguished.

I would recommend…
Get out of your little head,
Stop feeling sorry for yourself.
Continue Mission.

NUFF SAID.

January 27, 2021

Don't think I'm "special" when I beat you.

Never chalk victory up to my past or random circumstance.
The past doesn't amount to crap.
I pay the man daily.

The work sets me apart,
the willingness to suffer moves me further,
the sacrifice is what allows me to win.

*Do you not know that those who run in a race all run, but one
receives the prize? Run in such a way that you may obtain it.**

NUFF SAID.

1 Corinthians 9:24 NKJV

February 1, 2021

Might I ask… what's your problem?

I have been
Laughed at
Lied to
Stolen from
Disqualified
Cut open
Beat down
Humiliated
Left out
Told No
Failed
Stumbled
Lost
Broken
Hungry
Thirsty
Exhausted
Inadequate…

February 10, 2021

Yet I stand.

What's your problem?

Wherefore take unto you the whole armour of God, that ye may be able to withstand in the evil day, and having done all, to stand. *

NUFF SAID.

Ephesians 6:13 KJV

The victim says, The world is arrayed against me.

The victim says, I shall imprison myself with walls of anger, ignorance, and humanistic dependence.

The victim feels secure… until he falls in accordance with his pride.

The conqueror says, The world is arrayed against my King.

The conqueror says, I shall free myself with the fruits of love, long-suffering, and patience.

The conqueror feels secure… because his source of strength is inexhaustible and his King has overcome the world.

You choose… the victim vs. the conqueror.

NUFF SAID.

February 24, 2021

Hope is an ultimate thing.

This goes against the grain of the self-help and humanistic racket clogging your social media feed.

It is good for mankind to strive for a great and powerful experience in life, but ultimately the buck stops with the hope that remains when the vapor of your consciousness is fleeting.

You can receive all else that I teach, yet remain hopeless. There is only one message of hope I can offer you, and it is the foundation of my entire mission in life.

It is the simplest most perfect message ever created:
Find it at the cross of Jesus. Period.

NUFF SAID.

P.S. This is a photo of my grandfather during his last good day on earth. He passed through the veil of death with courage produced by hope provided by the cross.

March 2, 2021

Has the wool been pulled over your eyes, my dear sheep?
Were you led astray by loud talk and book deals?

Let me bring you back to reality.

Followers don't equal credibility.
Noise doesn't equal wisdom.

Volume doesn't equal strength.
Fame doesn't equal knowledge.

Lights and cameras don't equal work.
Your "stories" don't equal your reputation.

A victim's favorite costume is a wolf's clothing but the
victim's outward disguise can't hide the scent of his
weakness from the real wolves.

SHOW UP OR SHUT UP. No substitutes.

NUFF SAID.

March 15, 2021

Do you feel warm and fuzzy inside?

Being vulnerable isn't meant to make you feel comfy in your weakness; its purpose is to expose your inadequacy that you might own it and fix yourself immediately.

It still pays to be a winner, regardless of what your mommy told you.

NUFF SAID.

I don't care who's watching,
which is why others watch.

Being real is likely your greatest asset.

I worship not material things,
which is why abundant provision exists.

Obsession with the process is likely your quickest path to
financial gain.

My dues are paid,
which is why my ego doesn't limit my capacity.

Paying the man is likely the only way to free yourself from
the opinions of fools.

NUFF SAID.

March 25, 2021

I should have quit when I was told "No."
I should have found "another" path.
I should have tailored my objectives to accommodate the softness of society.

Except, I comprehend the process.
Except, I'm patient.
Except, I became proficient in adversity.

I suggest you do the same.

NUFF SAID.

March 28, 2021

About 3 of 7 Project

The number "3" in 3 of 7 Project stands for the 3 parts of every human—Body, Soul, Spirit. The number "7" represents the biblical number for completion.

Therefore, the mission of 3 of 7 Project is to teach you how to improve, maintain, and eventually master a strong physical body, a healthy soul (mind, will, and emotion), and a deep connection to the Creator of the universe, the God of the Bible, in order to become the most complete version of yourself.

Everyone involved with 3 of 7 Project is held to a high standard of personal excellence and required to daily practice what they preach.

3 of 7 Project offers in-person training opportunities to a limited number of applicants every year. All 3 of 7 Project live training programs are professionally designed to challenge your physical fitness, increase your mental toughness, and spur on deep thought about your spiritual life. 3 of 7 Project has set the industry standard for live training events year after year by constantly innovating and improving their course curriculum and environment.

You can also listen to the 3 of 7 Podcast, where we discuss all things body, soul, and spirit, on all major podcast platforms, or follow 3 of 7 Project on YouTube.

Find everything at www.3of7project.com.

NUFF SAID.

Made in the USA
Columbia, SC
05 July 2024

38112572R00072